BECOME A WINNER

365 ATHLETE'S MOTIVATIONAL QUOTES

BY

SCOTT OTERI

COPYRIGHT © 2015

Introduction

Everything is in your mind. Your ability to succeed, to fail, to win, to loose is just a matter of attitude. In this book, we have gathered quotations and words of wisdom from the most successful athlete's in the world.

They had the ability to overcome all the obstacles they had in their way to becoming great, and shared their thoughts about the things that pushed them forward.

Use this book and these words to overcome your fears and your negative thoughts. All the great ones had the will to win, and so should you. So relax, take this book, read it, and follow the path of victory.

1.

"It's not whether you get knocked down; it's whether you get up. "

- Vince Lombardi

2.

"The only way to prove that you're a good sport is to lose.
"

- Ernie Banks

3.

"Only he who can see the invisible can do the impossible.
"

– Frank L. Gaines

4.

"When you're riding, only the race in which you're riding is important. "

– Bill Shoemaker

5.

"Age is no barrier. It's a limitation you put on your mind."

– Jackie Joyner-Kersee

6.

"I always felt that my greatest asset was not my physical ability, it was my mental ability. "

– Bruce Jenner

7.

"A trophy carries dust. Memories last forever. "

– Mary Lou Retton

8.

"Number one is just to gain a passion for running. To love the morning, to love the trail, to love the pace on the track. And if some kid gets really good at it, that's cool too. "

– Pat Tyson

9.

"Most people give up just when they're about to achieve success. They quit on the one yard line. They give up at the last minute of the game one foot from a winning touchdown. "

– Ross Perot

10.

"You have to do something in your life that is honorable and not cowardly if you are to live in peace with yourself. "

– Larry Brown

11.

"There may be people that have more talent than you, but there is no excuse for anyone to work harder than you do. "

– Derek Jeter

12.

"Baseball is the only field of endeavor where a man can succeed three times out of ten and be considered a good performer. "

– Ted Williams

13.

"The five S's of sports training are: stamina, speed, strength, skill, and spirit; but the greatest of these is spirit. "

– Ken Doherty

14.

"An athlete cannot run with money in his pockets. He must run with hope in his heart and dreams in his head. "

– Emil Zatopek

15.

"When you've got something to prove, there's nothing greater than a challenge. "

– Terry Bradshaw

16.

"Never give up, never give in, and when the upper hand is ours, may we have the ability to handle the win with the dignity that we absorbed the loss. "

– Doug Williams

17.

"I've learned that something constructive comes from every defeat. "

- Tom Landry

18.

"Make sure your worst enemy doesn't live between your own two ears. "

– Laird Hamilton

19.

"Set your goals high, and don't stop till you get there. "

– Bo Jackson

20.

"I became a good pitcher when I stopped trying to make them miss the ball and started trying to make them hit it. "

– Sandy Koufax

21.

"If you can't outplay them, outwork them. "

– Ben Hogan

22.

"People ask me what I do in winter when there's no baseball. I'll tell you what I do. I stare out the window and wait for spring. "

– Rogers Hornsby

23.

"Most people never run far enough on their first wind to find out they've got a second. "

– William James

24.

"If at first you don't succeed, you are running about average. "

– M.H. Alderson

25.

"Continuous effort — not strength or intelligence — is the key to unlocking our potential. "

– Liane Cardes

26.

"Good is not good when better is expected. "

– Vin Scully

27.

"The difference between the impossible and the possible lies in a person's determination. "

– Tommy Lasorda

28.

"Champions keep playing until they get it right. "

– Billie Jean King

29.

"You were born to be a player. You were meant to be here. This moment is yours. "

– Herb Brooks

30.

"What you lack in talent can be made up with desire, hustle, and giving 110 percent all the time. "

– Don Zimmer

31.

"If you fail to prepare, you're prepared to fail. "

– Mark Spitz

32.

"How you respond to the challenge in the second half will determine what you become after the game, whether you are a winner or a loser. "

– Lou Holtz

33.

"Persistence can change failure into extraordinary achievement. "

– Matt Biondi

34.

"Sports serve society by providing vivid examples of excellence. "

– George F. Will

35.

"The principle is competing against yourself. It's about self-improvement, about being better than you were the day before. "

– Steve Young

36.

"The road to Easy Street goes through the sewer. "

– John Madden

37.

"You are never really playing an opponent. You are playing yourself, your own highest standards, and when you reach your limits, that is real joy. "

– Arthur Ashe

38.

"What makes something special is not just what you have to gain, but what you feel there is to lose. "

– Andre Agassi

39.

"The more difficult the victory, the greater the happiness in winning. "

– Pele

40.

"One man can be a crucial ingredient on a team, but one man cannot make a team. "

– Kareem Abdul-Jabbar

41.

"Nobody who ever gave his best regretted it. "

– George Halas

42.

"Stubbornness usually is considered a negative; but I think that trait has been a positive for me. " –

Cal Ripken Jr.

43.

"You've got to take the initiative and play your game. In a decisive set, confidence is the difference. "

– Chris Evert

44.

"When you win, say nothing, when you lose, say less. "

– Paul Brown

45.

"The hardest skill to acquire in this sport is the one where you compete all out, give it all you have, and you are still getting beat no matter what you do. When you have the killer instinct to fight through that, it is very special. "

– Eddie Reese

46.

"The mind is the limit. As long as the mind can envision the fact that you can do something, you can do it, as long as you really believe 100 percent. "

– Arnold Schwarzenegger

47.

"When I go out there, I have no pity on my brother. I am out there to win. "

– Joe Frazier

48.

"During my 18 years I came to bat almost 10,000 times. I struck out about 1,700 times and walked maybe 1,800 times. You figure a ballplayer will average about 500 at bats a season. That means I played seven years without ever hitting the ball. "

– Mickey Mantle

49.

"I never left the field saying I could have done more to get ready and that gives me piece of mind. "

– Peyton Manning

50.

"Leadership, like coaching, is fighting for the hearts and souls of men and getting them to believe in you. "

– Eddie Robinson

51.

"You win some, you lose some, and some get rained out, but you got to suit up for them all. "

– J. Askenberg

52.

"Always make a total effort, even when the odds are against you. "

– Arnold Palmer

53.

"Most talented players don't always succeed. Some don't even make the team. It's more what's inside. "

– Brett Favre

54.

"You have to expect things of yourself before you can do them. "

– Michael Jordan

55.

"You can motivate by fear, and you can motivate by reward. But both those methods are only temporary. The only lasting thing is self motivation. "

– Homer Rice

56.

"You find that you have peace of mind and can enjoy yourself, get more sleep, and rest when you know that it was a one hundred percent effort that you gave–win or lose. "

– Gordie Howe

57.

"My motto was always to keep swinging. Whether I was in a slump or feeling badly or having trouble off the field, the only thing to do was keep swinging. "

– Hank Aaron

58.

"I didn't believe in team motivation. I believe in getting a team prepared so it knows it will have the necessary confidence when it steps on the field and be prepared to play a good game. "

– Tom Landry

59.

"If you train hard, you'll not only be hard, you'll be hard to beat. "

– Herschel Walker

60.

"Your biggest opponent isn't the other guy. It's human nature. "

– Bobby Knight

61.

"If you don't have confidence, you'll always find a way not to win. "

– Carl Lewis

62.

"If you can believe it, the mind can achieve it. "

– Ronnie Lott

63.

"Obstacles don't have to stop you. If you run into a wall, don't turn around and give up. Figure out how to climb it, go through it, or work around it. "

– Michael Jordan

64.

"Make each day your masterpiece. "

– John Wooden

65.

"Excellence is the gradual result of always striving to do better. "

– Pat Riley

66.

"Win If You Can, Lose If You Must, But NEVER QUIT! "

– Cameron Trammell

67.

"If you have everything under control, you're not moving fast enough. "

– Mario Andretti

68.

"Push yourself again and again. Don't give an inch until the final buzzer sounds. "

– Larry Bird

69.

"If you aren't going all the way, why go at all? "

– Joe Namath

70.

"You can't put a limit on anything. The more you dream, the farther you get. "

– Michael Phelps

71.

"Do not let what you can not do interfere with what you can do. "

– John Wooden

72.

"Pain is temporary. It may last a minute, or an hour, or a day, or a year, but eventually it will subside and something else will take its place. If I quit, however, it lasts forever. "

– Lance Armstrong

73.

"Wisdom is always an overmatch for strength. "

– Phil Jackson

74.

"Some people say I have attitude – maybe I do…but I think you have to. You have to believe in yourself when no one else does – that makes you a winner right there. "

– Venus Williams

75.

"Never let the fear of striking out get in your way. "

– Babe Ruth

76.

"I hated every minute of training, but I said, 'Don't quit. Suffer now and live the rest of your life as a champion.' "

– Muhammad Ali

77.

"There are only two options regarding commitment. You're either IN or you're OUT. There is no such thing as life in-between. "

– Pat Riley

78.

"A champion is someone who gets up when he can't. "

– Jack Dempsey

79.

"It ain't over till it's over. "

– Yogi Berra

80.

"Never give up! Failure and rejection are only the first step to succeeding. "

– Jim Valvano

81.

"I've missed more than 9,000 shots in my career. I've lost almost 300 games. 26 times, I've been trusted to take the game winning shot and missed. I've failed over and over and over again in my life. And that is why I succeed. "

– Michael Jordan

82.

"You miss 100 percent of the shots you don't take. "

– Wayne Gretzky

83.

"The highest compliment that you can pay me is to say that I work hard every day, that I never dog it. "

– Wayne Gretzky

84.

"Gold medals aren't really made of gold. They're made of sweat, determination, and a hard-to-find alloy called guts. "

– Dan Gable

85.

"The way a team plays as a whole determines its success. You may have the greatest bunch of individual stars in the world, but if they don't play together, the club won't be worth a dime. "

- Babe Ruth

86.

"If you think it's hard to meet new people, try picking up the wrong golf ball. "

- Jack Lemmon

87.

"Every day is a new opportunity. You can build on yesterday's success or put its failures behind and start over again. That's the way life is, with a new game every day, and that's the way baseball is. "

- Bob Feller

88.

"Just play. Have fun. Enjoy the game. "

- Michael Jordan

89.

"Winners never quit and quitters never win. "

- Vince Lombardi

90.

"Success is where preparation and opportunity meet. "

- Bobby Unser

91.

"Many men go fishing all of their lives without knowing that it is not fish they are after. "

- Henry David Thoreau

92.

"It's just a job. Grass grows, birds fly, waves pound the sand. I beat people up. "

- Muhammad Ali

93.

"Sports do not build character. They reveal it. "

- Heywood Broun

94.

"A good hockey player plays where the puck is. A great hockey player plays where the puck is going to be. "

- Wayne Gretzky

95.

"To me, it doesn't matter how good you are. Sport is all about playing and competing. Whatever you do in cricket and in sport, enjoy it, be positive and try to win. "

- Ian Botham

96.

"You can't put a limit on anything. The more you dream, the farther you get. "

- Michael Phelps

97.

"You can't win unless you learn how to lose. "

- Kareem Abdul-Jabbar

98.

"Don't look back. Something might be gaining on you. "

- Satchel Paige

99.

"One man practicing sportsmanship is far better than a hundred teaching it. "

- Knute Rockne

100.

"Adversity causes some men to break; others to break records. "

- William Arthur Ward

101.

"If winning isn't everything, why do they keep score? "

- Vince Lombardi

102.

"Just be patient. Let the game come to you. Don't rush. Be quick, but don't hurry. "

- Earl Monroe

103.

"Winning is habit. Unfortunately, so is losing. "

- Vince Lombardi

104.

"Approach the game with no preset agendas and you'll probably come away surprised at your overall efforts. "

- Phil Jackson

105.

"Show me a good loser, and I'll show you a loser. "

- Vince Lombardi

106.

"Nobody's a natural. You work hard to get good and then work to get better. It's hard to stay on top. "

- Paul Coffey

107.

"If a man can beat you, walk him. "

- Satchel Paige

108.

"Be strong in body, clean in mind, lofty in ideals. "

- James Naismith

109.

"When you see a good move, look for a better one. "

- Emanuel Lasker

110.

"The beauty of a move lies not in its' appearance but in the thought behind it. "

- Aron Nimzowitsch

111.

"Show me a good and gracious loser and I'll show you a failure. "

- Knute Rockne

112.

"No one ever won a game by resigning. "

- Ksawery Tartakower

113.

"Strategy requires thought,tactics require observation. "

- Machgielis "Max " Euwe

114.

"You can learn a line from a win and a book from a defeat. "

- Paul Brown

115.

"Aim for the sky and you'll reach the ceiling. Aim for the ceiling and you'll stay on the floor. "

- Bill Shankly

116.

"Natural abilities are like natural plants; they need pruning by study. "

- Arnold Jacob "Red " Auerbach

117.

"It is better to fail aiming high than to succeed aiming low. "

- William Edward "Bill " Nicholson

118.

"A winner never stops trying. "

- Tom Landry

119.

"It is useless to put on your brakes when you're upside down. "

- Paul Leonard Newman

120.

"Concentration comes out of a combination of confidence and hunger. "

- Arnold Daniel Palmer

121.

"The man who can drive himself further once the effort gets painful is the man who will win. "

- Sir Roger Gilbert Bannister

122.

"Success is not forever and failure isn't fatal. "

- Donald Francis "Don " Shula

123.

"Success for an athlete follows many years of hard work and dedication. "

– Michael Diamond

124.

"My attitude is that if you push me towards a weakness, I will turn that weakness into a strength. "

– Michael Jordan

125.

"I've got a theory that if you give 100% all of the time, somehow things will work out in the end. "

– Larry Bird

126.

"Good, better, best. Never let it rest. Until your good is better and your better is best. "

– Tim Duncan

127.

"Talent is never enough. With few exceptions the best players are the hardest workers. "

– Magic Johnson

128.

"If you are afraid of failure you don't deserve to be successful! "

– Charles Barkley

129.

"You can't get much done in life if you only work on the days when you feel good. "

– Jerry West

130.

"Basketball doesn't build character. It reveals it. "

– Unknown

131.

"Show me a guy who's afraid to look bad, and I'll show you a guy you can beat every time. "

– Lou Brock

132.

"Just keep going. Everybody gets better if they keep at it. "

– Ted Williams

133.

"Never let your head hang down. Never give up and sit down and grieve. Find another way. "

– Satchel Paige

134.

"It ain't over till it's over. "

– Yogi Berra

135.

"There may be people that have more talent than you, but there's no excuse for anyone to work harder than you do.
"

– Derek Jeter

136.

"It's hard to beat a person who never gives up. "

– Babe Ruth

137.

"Without self-discipline, success is impossible, period. "

– Lou Holtz

138.

"Do you know what my favorite part of the game is? The opportunity to play. "

– Mike Singletary

139.

"You're never a loser until you quit trying. "

– Mike Ditka

140.

"The quality of a person's life is in direct proportion to their commitment to excellence, regardless of their chosen field of endeavor. "

– Vince Lombardi

141.

"Today I will do what others won't, so tomorrow I can accomplish what others can't. "

– Jerry Rice

142.

"Success is no accident. It is hard work, perseverance, learning, sacrifice and most of all, love for what you are doing or learning to do. "

– Pele

143.

"If you only ever give 90% in training then you will only ever give 90% when it matters. "

– Michael Owen

144.

"If a team wants to intimidate you physically and you let them, they've won. "

– Mia Hamm

145.

"It is more difficult to stay on top than to get there. "

– Mia Hamm

146.

"The vision of a champion is someone who is bent over, drenched in sweat, at the point of exhaustion, when no one else is watching. "

– Anson Dorrance

147.

"If we perform as a unit and if every single player gives it his very best, everything can happen. "

– Oliver Kahn

148.

"Everything is practice. "

– Bill Shankley

149.

"I am building a fire, and everyday I train, I add more fuel. At just the right moment, I light the match. "

– Mia Hamm

150.

"The fight is won or lost far away from witnesses – behind the lines, in the gym, and out there on the road, long before I dance under those lights. "

– Muhammad Ali

151.

"He who is not courageous enough to take risks will accomplish nothing in life. "

– Muhammad Ali

152.

"It is not the size of a man but the size of his heart that matters. "

– Evander Holyfield

153.

"The highest compliment that you can pay me is to say that I work hard every day. "

– Wayne Gretzky

154.

"Procrastination is one of the most common and deadliest of diseases and its toll on success and happiness is heavy. "

– Wayne Gretzky

155.

"The wisdom acquired with the passage of time is a useless gift unless you share it. "

– Esther Williams

156.

"You have to train your mind like you train your body. "

– Bruce Jenner

157.

"This ability to conquer oneself is no doubt the most precious of all things sports bestows. "

– Olga Korbut

158.

"Each of us has a fire in our hearts for something. It's our goal in life to find it and keep it lit. "

– Mary Lou Retton

159.

"It took me time to realize that the men who won Olympic gold medals in the decathlon are just men, just like me. "

– Dan O'Brien

160.

"Concentration is why some athletes are better than others. You develop that concentration in training and concentrate in a meet. "

– Edwin Moses

161.

"Mental will is a muscle that needs exercise, just like muscles of the body. "

– Lynn Jennings

162.

"I know what I have to do, and I'm going to do whatever it takes. If I do it, I'll come out a winner, and it doesn't matter what anyone else does. "

– Florence Griffith Joyner

163.

"To give any less than your best is to sacrifice a gift. "

– Steve Prefontaine

164.

"Run when you can, walk if you have to, crawl if you must; just never give up. "

– Dean Karnazes

165.

"It's all about the journey, not the outcome. "

– Carl Lewis

166.

"Never underestimate the power of dreams and the influence of the human spirit. The potential for greatness lives within each of us. "

– Wilma Rudolph

167.

"When I race my mind is full of doubts – who will finish second, who will finish third? "

– Noureddine Morceli

168.

"To uncover your true potential you must first find your own limits and then you have to have the courage to blow past them. "

– Picabo Street

169.

"Strength does not come from winning. Your struggles develop your strengths. "

– Arnold Schwarzenegger

170.

"We must train hard. It's not about denying a weakness may exist but about denying its right to persist. "

– Vince McConnell

171.

"If it doesn't challenge you, it won't change you. " –

Fred Devito

172.

"Under pressure you can perform fifteen percent better or worse. "

– Scott Hamilton

173.

"If you dream and you allow yourself to dream you can do anything. "

– Clara Hughes

174.

"Follow your dreams, work hard, practice and persevere. Get plenty of exercise and maintain a healthy lifestyle. "

– Sasha Cohen

175.

"Competing at the highest level is the greatest test of one's character. "

– Russell Mark

176.

"Every time you sleep in, every time you miss a workout, you make it that much easier for me to beat you. "

– Unknown

177.

"If good luck exist, it is that which results from hard work and preparation. "

– Unknown

178.

"You can have results or you can have your excuses. You cannot have both. "

– Unknown

179.

"Obsessed is just a word the lazy use to describe the dedicated. "

– Unknown

180.

"The man who cannot believe in himself cannot believe in anything else. "

– Unknown

181.

"We create success or failure on the course primarily by our thoughts. "

- Gary Player

182.

"Great moments are born from great opportunities. "

- Herbert Paul Brooks, Jr.

183.

"Start where you are. Use what you have. Do what you can. "

- Arthur Robert Ashe, Jr.

184.

"The strength of the team is each individual member. The strength of each member is the team. "

- Philip Douglas "Phil " Jackson

185.

"You don't have to have been a horse to be a jockey. "

- Arrigo Sacchi

186.

"Every disadvantage has its advantage. "

- Hendrik Johannes Cruijff

187.

"Every defeat is a victory in itself. "

- Francisco Maturana García

188.

"To be great we need to win games we aren't supposed to win. "

- Julius Winfield Erving II

189.

"You win some, lose some, and wreck some. "

- Ralph Dale Earnhardt, Sr.

190.

"To finish first, you must first finish. "

- Rick Ravon Mears

191.

"It is better to win ten times 1-0 than to win once 10-0. "

- Vahid "Vaha " Halilhodžic'

192.

"You don't win championships by just being normal, by just being average. "

- William Theodore "Bill " Walton III

193.

"Ask not what your teammates can do for you. Ask what you can do for your teammates. "

- Earvin "Magic " Johnson, Jr.

194.

"Getting to the top is optional. Getting down is mandatory. "

- Edmund Viesturs

195.

"Money does not guarantee success. "

- Jose Mourinho

196.

"Pain is nothing. Pain is in the mind. If you can walk you can run."

-Cameron Michael Neely

197.

"You can't afford to live your life with regrets. "- Shane Keith Warne

198.

"No matter how good you get, you can always get better and that's the exciting part. "

- Eldrick Tont "Tiger " Woods

199.

"Hard work beats talent when talent fails to work hard. "

- Kevin Wayne Durant

200.

"There are no shortcuts to any place worth going. "

- Beverly Sills

201.

"You only ever grow as a human being if you're outside your comfort zone. "

- Percy Cerutty

202.

"It is only through work and strife that either nation or individual moves on to greatness. The great man is always the man of mighty effort, and usually the man whom grinding need has trained to mighty effort. "

- Theodore Roosevelt

203.

"The turning point in the process of growing up is when you discover the core of strength within you that survives all hurt. "

- Max Lerner

204.

"Spirit ... has fifty times the strength and staying power of brawn and muscle. "

- Unknown

205.

"Train, don't strain. "

- Arthur Lydiard

206.

"You would fain be victor at the Olympic Games, you say. Yes, but weigh the conditions, weigh the consequences; then and then only, lay to your hand-if it be for your profit. You must live by rule, submit to diet, abstain from dainty meats, exercise your body perforce at stated hours, in heat or in cold; drink no cold water, nor, it may be, wine. In a word, you must surrender yourself wholly to your trainer, as though to a physician. "

- Epictetus, (c.A.D. 50-c.A.D. 138)

207.

"Just remember this: No one ever won the olive wreath with an impressive training diary. "

- Marty Liquori

208.

"The more I talk to athletes, the more convinced I become that the method of training is relatively unimportant. There are many ways to the top, and the training method you choose is just the one that suits you best. No, the important thing is the attitude of the athlete, the desire to get to the top. "

- Herb Elliott

209.

"Restlessness is discontent - and discontent is the first necessity of progress. Show me a thoroughly satisfied man - and I will show you a failure. "

- Thomas Alva Edison

210.

"My jump was imperfect, my run-in was too short and my hands were too far back at takeoff. When I manage to iron out these faults, I am sure I can improve. "

- Sergei Bubka

211.

"Fall seven times, stand up eight. "

- Japanese proverb

212.

"Only those who risk going to far can possibly find out how far one can go. "

- T.S. Eliot

213.

"Daring ideas are like chessmen moved forward; they may be beaten, but they may start a winning game. "

- Johann Wolfgang von Goethe

214.

"Man cannot discover new oceans unless he has the courage to lose sight of the shore. "

- Andre Gide

215.

"Inspiration cannot be willed, though it can be wooed. "

- Anthony Storr

216.

"Problems are only opportunities in work clothes. "

- Henry J. Kaiser

217.

"Nothing will work unless you do. "

- John Wooden

218.

"Everything you want is out there waiting for you to ask. Everything you want also wants you. But you have to take action to get it. "

- Jack Canfield

219.

"If you want to be the best, work harder than the rest. If you don't want to be the best, just work like the rest. "

- Robert Stinson

220.

"Impossible is just a big word thrown around by small men who find it easier to live in the world they've been given than to explore the power they have to change it. Impossible is not a fact. It's an opinion. Impossible is not a declaration. It's a dare. Impossible is potential. Impossible is temporary. Impossible is nothing."

– Muhammad Ali

221.

"Talent is God given. Be humble. Fame is man-given. Be grateful. Conceit is self-given. Be careful."

– John Wooden

222.

"What do you do with a mistake: recognize it, admit it, learn from it, forget it."

– Dean Smith

223.

"Somewhere behind the athlete you've become and the hours of practice and the coaches who have pushed you is a little girl who fell in love with the game and never looked back… play for her."

– Mia Hamm

224.

"God places the heaviest burden on those who can carry its weight."

– Reggie White

225.

"If you play your heart out for what your jersey says on the front, everyone will remember what the jersey says on the back."

– Miracle

226.

"Heroes get remembered, but legends never die."

– Babe Ruth

227.

"Skill and confidence are an unconquered army. "

- George Herbert

228.

"Victory belongs to the most persevering."

- Napoleon Bonaparte

229.

"Maybe the day will come when I can sit back and be content....But until that day comes, I intend to stay in the batter's box — I don't let the big guys push me out of there anymore — and keep hammering away. "

- Hank Aaron

230.

"You are the handicap you must face. You are the one who must choose your place. "

- James Lane Allen

231.

"It isn't hard to be good from time to time in sports. What's tough is being good every day."

- Willie Mays

232.

"Sports serve society by providing vivid examples of excellence."

- George F. Will

233.

"There are no gains without pains. "

- Adlai Stevenson

234.

"To win without risk is to triumph without glory. "

- Corneille

235.

"They will rise highest who strive for the highest place. "

- Latin Proverb

236.

"Nothing succeeds like success."

- Proverb

237.

"The moment of victory is much too short to live for that and nothing else."

– Martina Navratilova

238.

"If it is a cliché to say athletics build character as well as muscle, then I subscribe to the cliché. "

– Gerald Ford

239.

"Sports gives your life structure, discipline, and a pure fulfillment that few other areas of endeavor provide. "

– Bob Cousy

240.

"I never thought about losing, but now that it's happened, the only thing is to do it right. "

– Muhammad Ali

241.

"Dictators lead through fear; good coaches do not. "

– John Wooden

242.

"The will must be stronger than the skill. "

– Muhammed Ali

243."

Always imitate the behavior of the winner when you lose.
"

— Anonymous

244.

"It's not up to anyone else to make me give my best. "

– Hakeem Olajuwon

245.

"If all I'm remembered for is being a good basketball player, then I've done a bad job with the rest of my life. "

– Isiah Thomas

246.

"Ain't no man can avoid being born average, but there ain't no man got to be common."

-Satchel Paige

247.

"When the game is over, it is really just beginning. "

– Jerry Kramer

248.

"The harder you work, the luckier you get. "

– Gary Player

249.

"The speed of a runaway horse counts for nothing. "

– Jean Cocteau

250.

"It's never crowded along the extra mile. "

– Wayne Dyer

251.

"Start by doing what is necessary, then do what is possible, and suddenly you are doing the impossible. "

– St. Francis of Assisi

252.

"It is normal to enjoy praise and dislike criticism. True character is when you prevent either from affecting you in a negative matter. "

– John Wooden

253.

"What it comes down to is that anybody can win with the best horse. What makes you good is if you can take the second- or third-best horse and win. "

– Vicky Aragon

254.

"Thank God for competition. When our competitors upset our plans or outdo our designs, they open infinite possibilities of our own work to us. "

– Gil Atkinson

255.

"I love the winning, I can take the losing. But most of all, I love to play. "

– Boris Becker

256.

"Somebody will always break your records. It is how you live that counts. "

– Earl Campbell

257.

"Everybody pulls for David; nobody roots for Goliath. "

– Wilt Chamberlain

258.

"It's amazing how much of this is mental. Everybody's in good shape. Everybody knows how to ski. Everybody has good equipment. When it really boils down to it, it's who wants it the most and who's the most confident. "

– Reggie Crist

259.

"You get out in front – you stay out in front. "

– A. J. Foy

260.

"Every time you go out on the ice, there are slight flaws. You can always think of something you should have done better. These are the things you must work on. "

– Dorothy Hamill

261.

"I play with friends sometimes, but there are never friendly games. "

– Ben Hogan

262.

"The biggest things are often the easiest to do because there is so little competition. "

– William Van Horne

263.

"Do your work with your whole heart and you will succeed – there's so little competition. "

– Elbert Hubbard

264.

"Running for money doesn't make you run fast. It makes you run first. "

– Ben Jipcho

265.

"Masculinity is not something given to you, but something you gain. And you gain it by winning small battles with honor. "

– Norman Mailer

266.

"Winning is about heart, not just legs. It's got to be in the right place. "

– Lance Armstrong

267.

"The integrity and self-esteem gained from winning the battle against extremity are the richest treasures in my life "

– Diana Nyad

268.

"Every strike brings me closer to the next home run."

— Babe Ruth

269.

"The mastery of the true self, and the refusal to permit others to dominate us, is the ultimate in living and self-expression in athletics. "

– Percy Cerutty

270.

"The score never interested me, only the game."

— Mae West

271.

"A player who conjugates a verb in the first-person singular cannot be part of the squad. He has to conjugate the verb in the first-person plural. We. "

– Vanderlei Luxemburgo da Silva

272.

"Victory has a thousand fathers, but defeat is an orphan. "

– John F. Kennedy

273.

"When building a team, I always search first for people who love to win. If I can't find any of those, I look for people who hate to lose. "

– H. Ross Perot

274.

"It's not my job to motivate players. They bring extraordinary motivation to our program. It's my job not to de-motivate them. "

–Lou Holtz

275.

"You can stand tall without standing on someone. You can be a victor without having victims. "

– Harriet Woods

276.

"Tactics, fitness, stroke ability, adaptability, experience, and sportsmanship are all necessary for winning. "–

Fred Perry

277.

"No pain, no palm; no thorns, no throne; no gall, no glory; no cross, no crown. "

– William Penn

278.

"When you want to win a game, you have to teach. When you lose a game, you have to learn. "

– Tom Landry

279.

"Sports events do not really exist at all unless there is a certain order and fairness – justice in each event. "

– Michael Novak

280.

"Give me 25 guys on the last year of their contracts and I'll win a pennant every year. "

– Sparky Anderson

281.

"Three failures denote uncommon strength. A weakling has not enough grit to fail thrice. "

– Minna Thomas Antrim

282.

"If character is what you do when no one is watching, then sportsmanship is that conduct with everybody watching. "

– Bob Ley

283.

"If we win or lose this weekend, it will not make a difference in our lives. But why we play and how we play will make a difference in our lives forever. "

– Beth Anders

284.

"Great things are done when men and mountains meet. "

– William Blake

285.

"A pat on the back is only a few vertebrae removed from a kick in the pants, but is miles ahead in results. "

– Ella Wheeler Wilcox

286.

"The successful warrior is the average man – with laser-like focus. "

– Bruce Lee

287.

"I do not try to dance better than anyone else. I only try to dance better than myself. "

– Mikhail Baryshnikov

288.

"Nothing focuses the mind better than the constant sight of a competitor who wants to wipe you off the map. "

– Wayne Calloway

289.

"Class is when they run you out of town and it looks like you're leading a parade. "

– Bill Battle

290.

"Always keep your composure. You can't score from the penalty box. "

– Bobby Hull

291.

"No one has ever drowned in sweat. "

– Lou Holtz

292.

"Life will always throw you curves. Just keep fouling them off. The right pitch will come. When it does, be prepared to run the bases. "

– Rick Maksian

293.

"It is always your next move. "

– Napoleon Hill

294.

"Let your performance do the thinking. "

– H. Jackson Brown, Jr

295.

"Man is so made that when anything fires his soul, impossibilities vanish. "

– Jean de La Fontaine

296.

"Action springs not from thought, but from a readiness for responsibility. "

– Dietrich Bonhoeffer

297.

"At one point in your life, you either have the thing you want or the reasons why you don't. "

–Andy Roddick

298.

"Be an all-out, not a hold-out. "–

Norman Vincent Peale

299.

"My mother taught me to believe I could achieve any accomplishment. The first was to walk without braces. "

– Wilma Rudoph

300.

"If you want to find the real competition, just look in the mirror. After awhile you'll see your rivals scrambling for second place."

— Criss Jami

301.

"The secret of winning football games is working as a team. I play not my 11 best, but my best 11. "

– Knute Rockne

302.

"I feel the need to endanger myself every so often."

— Tim Daly

303.

"Most people achieved their greatest success one step beyond what looked like their greatest failure. "

– Brian Tracy

304.

"In the dust of defeat as well as the laurels of victory there is a glory to be found if one has done his best."

— Eric Liddell

305.

"Whether you think you can or think you can't, you're right. "

– Henry Ford

306.

"Perseverance is not a long race; it is many short races one after another. "

– Walter Elliott

307.

"Others can stop you temporarily. You are the only one who can do it permanently. "

– Zig Ziglar

308.

"You always pass failure on the way to success. "

– Mickey Rooney

309.

"A hero is one who knows how to hang on one minute longer. "

– Norwegian proverb

310.

"One that desires to excel should endeavor in those things that are in themselves most excellent. "

– Epictetus

311.

"One machine can do the work of 50 ordinary men. No machine can do the work of one extraordinary man. "

– Elbert Hubbard

312.

"You can discover more about a person in an hour of play than a year of conversation. "

– Plato

313.

"Behind all the years of practice and all the hours of glory waits that inexorable terror of living without the game. "

– Bill Bradley

314.

"If you're losing a tug of war with a tiger, give it the rope. You can always buy a new one. "

–Max Gunther

315.

"When I did this three years ago, it was like death. When I did it last year, it was like near death. This year, it was just really hard. "

– John Howie

316.

"However beautiful the strategy, you should occasionally look at the results. "

– Winston Churchill

317.

"Experience is a hard teacher because she gives the test first, the lesson afterward. "

– Vernon Law

318.

"No amount of ability is of the slightest avail without honor. "

– Andrew Carnegie

319.

"We must all suffer one of two things: the pain of discipline or the pain of disappointment. "

– Jim Rohn

320.

"Cards are war in disguise of a sport. "

– Charles Lamb

321.

"What are we at the park for except to win? I'd trip my mother. I'd help her up, brush her off, tell her I'm sorry. But mother don't make it to third. "

– Leo Durocher

322.

"In the arena of human life, the honors and rewards fall to those who show their good qualities in action. "

– Aristotle

323.

"There is no quality of human nature so nearly royal as the ability to yield gracefully. "

– Charles Conrad

324.

"It is necessary for us to learn from others' mistakes. You will not live long enough to make them all yourself. "

–Hyman G. Rickover

325.

"There are many victories worse than a defeat. "

– George Eliot

326.

"Success without honor is an unseasoned dish. It will satisfy your hunger, but it won't taste good. "

– Joe Paterno

327.

"If you can't win, make the one ahead of you break the record. "

– Jan McKeithen

328.

"Nothing can stop the man with the right mental attitude from achieving his goal; nothing can help the man with the wrong mental attitude. "

– W. W. Ziege

329.

"Success isn't based on your ability to change. It is based on your ability to change faster than your competition. "

– Mark Sanborn

330.

"Stay true to yourself and listen to your inner voice. It will lead you to your dream."

— James Ross

331.

"A leader not only stays above the line between right and wrong, he stays well clear of the gray areas. "

– G. Alan Bernard

332.

"I'm the best there is, the best there was, and the best there ever will be."

— Bret Hart

333.

"If you're not working at your game to the utmost of your ability, someone out there with equal ability is. And one day you'll play each other. "

– "Easy" Ed Macauley

334.

"The man who complains about the way the ball bounces is likely the one who dropped it. "

– Lou Holt

335.

"Concentration is the ability to think about absolutely nothing when it is absolutely necessary. "

–Ray Knight

336.

"Those who know how to win are much more numerous than those who know how to make proper use of their victories. "

– Polybius

337.

"Everything you need is already inside."

— Bill Bowerman

338.

"The only problem with success is it doesn't teach you how to deal with failure. "

– Tommy Lasorda

339.

"Never let defeat have the last word. "

– Tibetan proverb

340.

"If anything goes bad, I did it. If anything goes semi-good, we did it. If anything goes really good, you did it. That's all it takes to get people to win football games for you. "

– Paul "Bear" Bryant

341.

"Never mind what others do; do better than yourself. Beat your own record from day to day and you are a success. "

– William J.H. Boetcker

342.

"Obstacles are those frightful things you see when you take your eyes off your goal. "

– Henry Ford

343.

"The finish line is sometimes merely the symbol of victory. All sorts of personal triumphs take place before that point, and the outcome may be decided long before the end. "

– Laurence Malone

344.

"Leaders are like eagles – they don't flock. You find them one at a time. "

– Knute Rockne

345.

"No matter how hard the loss, defeat might serve as well as victory to shape the soul and let the glory out. "

– Al Gore

346.

"I became an optimist when I discovered I wasn't going to win any more games by being anything else. "

– Earl Weaver

347.

"The only disability in life is a bad attitude. "

– Scott Hamilton

348.

"The best motivation always comes from within."

- Michael Johnson

349.

"Money was never a big motivation for me, except as a way to keep score. The real excitement is playing the game."

- Donald Trump

350.

"To succeed…You need to find something to hold on to, something to motivate you, something to inspire you."

- Tony Dorsett

351.

"It isn't the mountains ahead to climb that wear you out; it's the pebble in your shoe. "

-Muhammad Ali

352.

"Difficulties in life are intended to make us better, not bitter. "

- Dan Reeves

353.

"Failures are finger posts on the road to achievement. "

- Charles F. Kettering

354.

"A team is where a boy can prove his courage on his own. A gang is where a coward goes to hide. "

- Mickey Mantle

355.

"The rewards are going to come, but my happiness is just loving the sport and having fun performing."

- Jackie Joyner Kersee

356.

"Don't tell me how rocky the sea is, just bring the ship in.
"

- Lou Holtz

357.

"I was told over and over again that I would never be successful, that I was not going to be competitive and the technique was simply not going to work. All I could do was shrug and say "We'll just have to see."

-Dick Fosbury

358.

"Know yourself and you will win all battles. "

- Lao Tzu

359.

"Confidence comes not from always being right but from not fearing to be wrong. "

- Peter T. McIntyre

360.

"Even if you are on the right track, you will get run over if you just sit there. "

- Will Rogers

361.

"Sweat is the cologne of accomplishment. "

- Heywood Hale Broun

362.

"Toughness is in the soul and spirit, not in muscles. "

- Alex Karras

363.

"Luck? Sure. But only after long practice and only with the ability to think under pressure. "

- Babe Didrikson Zaharias

364.

"My thoughts before a big race are usually pretty simple. I tell myself: Get out of the blocks, run your race, stay relaxed. If you run your race, you'll win... channel your energy. Focus. "

- Carl Lewis

365.

"You can always become better."

– Tiger Woods

www.ingramcontent.com/pod-product-compliance
Lightning Source LLC
Chambersburg PA
CBHW050411290526
45786CB00003B/1210